THE HOSPIT
ST CRC

The Master's Welcome

The Hospital of St Cross is far more than a lovely collection of old buildings and part of our national heritage. It is a living institution which offers a haven for elderly gentlemen. Most of us think that sheltered accommodation is a modern idea: the Hospital of St Cross has been providing it for 800 years!

The Brothers who live here today are the successors of the original poor men of 1136. Every day since then, Brothers have worshipped in the fine Norman church which dominates the Hospital, and have in their turn offered hospitality to the parishioners of St Faith's for whom the church has been the centre of worship for over 450 years.

The Hospital has not always been the tranquil, timeless haven it is today: history and legend tell of abundant dark deeds and mysterious events. We hope that this book will give you an insight into the fascinating, often turbulent story of the Hospital of St Cross and that your visit here proves peaceful and enriching.

Tony Outhwaite

MASTER OF ST CROSS

> 'Thirteen poor men, feeble and so reduced in strength that they can scarcely, or not at all, support themselves without other aid, shall remain in the same Hospital constantly; to whom necessary clothing, provided by the Prior of the establishment, shall be given, and beds fit for their infirmities; and daily a good loaf of wheaten bread of the weight of five measures, three dishes at dinner, and one for supper, and drink in sufficient quantity ...
>
> And besides these thirteen poor men, one hundred other poor persons, as deserving as can be found and more indigent, shall be received at the hour of dinner...'
>
> THE CHARTER OF FOUNDATION

O ut of one man's dream to help others who were starving was created the Hospital of St Cross, Britain's oldest existing charitable institution and surely the most beautiful group of medieval buildings still in use. The Hospital was the achievement of Henry de Blois, King Stephen's half-brother and grandson of William the Conqueror. Young, wealthy and powerful, de Blois was monk, knight and politician in one. Appointed Bishop of Winchester in 1129 at the age of 28, he soon came to resent his subservience to the Archbishops of Canterbury and York. He therefore set about building a power base to persuade the King to create a third West Country archdiocese with himself at the head.

Between 1133 and 1136, de Blois founded the Hospital of St Cross (*sancta crux*) in the Itchen water meadows near Sparkford. The almshouses were funded by tithes from 15 Hampshire parishes and donations from elsewhere. One Sussex parish had to provide the Hospital annually with a dolphin!

BELOW: *This engraving of a 12th-century enamelled plaque (in the British Museum) is thought to show Henry de Blois presenting to Winchester Cathedral a new receptacle for the bones of St Swithun. De Blois rebuilt the cathedral tower, created three local Bishop's palaces, seven castles and also, it is thought, Romsey Abbey.*

St Cross served a wide area around it. The fact that the 'hundred other poor persons' could take away with them what they did not eat in the Hundred Men's Hall, meant that 100 families, not just 100 people, were being helped in the struggle to survive. In the early 1100s Winchester probably had around 5,000 inhabitants. Thus a considerable portion of the population came to rely on de Blois' foundation for sustenance. This tradition endured almost continuously until the late 1800s.

The work of St Cross was well known. People sought to become Brothers or to obtain places for their friends. Samuel Johnson, for example, wrote in 1777 asking that a friend of his, who suffered from palsy, should be admitted.

The wealth and importance of St Cross caused it to be regarded with envious eyes. Kings, archbishops and bishops all used it to further their own or their family's fortunes, the fate of many medieval institutions. For most of the time, however, the Hospital carried out its duties of caring for 13 poor men, though occasionally the 100 poor men were on short commons.

The warmth of compassion and care we can sense within the Charter of Foundation is very strongly echoed in the comfortable friendly haven that St Cross is today. But greed and corruption have played a part in its long history.

In 1151, in an attempt to guarantee future financial security for the Hospital, de Blois put St Cross into the hands of the Knights Hospitallers of St John of Jerusalem, an organization of crusaders who poured vast resources into protecting the routes of pilgrimage through Europe to the Holy Land. But the Hospital's income went in the wrong direction. Successive Bishops became dissatisfied with the fact that the Knights were bleeding the Hospital of its funds. Building work on the church stopped as control was wrested to and fro. It took a Papal Commission to hand the Hospital finally back to the Bishops of Winchester, and in 1204 building began again.

But things were still not as they should have been. Some Bishops installed relatives as Masters who stayed away but drew large amounts from the Hospital's tithes. Other Bishops would attempt to remove those unfit for office. Bishop de Stratford, referring to one Master, Peter de Galiciano, wrote that he 'had misapplied the rents and profits of the House … to the known dilapidation of the goods of the said House and subtraction of the alms.' Occasionally kings would intervene, but not always on the side of justice.

> *'Then was corn dear, and flesh, and cheese, and butter, for there was none in the land; wretched men starved with hunger – some lived on alms who had been erstwhile rich… The earth bore no corn; one might as well have tilled the sea… It was said that Christ and His saints slept.'*
>
> THE ENGLISH CHRONICLE FOR THE YEAR 1137

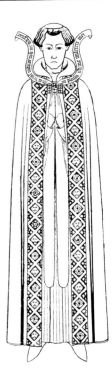

ir Roger de Cloune (1370–74) was a particularly notorious Master, combining greed with criminal acumen. Bishop Wykeham discovered that not only had de Cloune pulled the larder down, ordered replacement materials and sold them off for his own gain, but had turned out most of the Brethren and reduced the 100 men feeding heartily in the hall to two or three begging scraps at the gate. By selling off as much property as he could, de Cloune had virtually destroyed the Hospital before he was finally ousted.

Appointed Master in 1382, John de Campeden, with Wykeham's active assistance, quickly put to rights what had been damaged. In five years he rebuilt the church tower and renovated the interior, fitting new stalls and a high altar. In 1390, 255 years after it was started, the Foundation of St Cross as originally conceived was complete.

One of the leading figures in the Hospital's history was Cardinal Henry Beaufort, for 33 years Bishop of Winchester and four times Chancellor of England. In his later years, he became interested in the Hospital, proposing in 1446 a scheme to add another almshouse for former servants of the state, of noble birth but now living in poverty. The Wars of the Roses put an end to the plan when the Yorkist victors took the lands which would have endowed the new foundation.

Forty years after Beaufort's death, an 'almshouse of Noble Poverty' was founded with one chaplain and two Brothers. To this day Brothers of the Beaufort foundation wear red gowns with a cardinal's badge.

The 1530s saw the Hospital survive unscathed the period of Dissolution. St Cross received a visitation from Leigh, one of Thomas Cromwell's feared team, but it was proved that, as a lay foundation, the Hospital did not come under the terms of the Act of Suppression.

During the next 300 years many Masters of varying degrees of honesty came and went. One of the best was William Lewis (1628–69). His years of rebuilding were interrupted by the

RIGHT: *The 15th-century Beaufort Tower, formerly part of the Master's lodging. The statue of the Madonna and Child replaced one which fell down c.1750. It is thought that Cardinal Beaufort may have become active in the Hospital's affairs as a penance for his part in the trial and execution of Joan of Arc.*

ABOVE RIGHT: *The outline of a brass in the church depicting John de Campeden, Master 1382–1410. A small stone in the floor of the nave aisle is thought to commemorate his death.*

RIGHT: *A quiet corner of the Brothers' quarters.*

forcible introduction of two lay Masters, Lisle and Cooke, during the Commonwealth, but at the Restoration of Charles II, Lewis was also restored to continue his good work.

The most notorious Master of more recent times was Francis North, later Earl of Guildford, who acquired the job in 1807 through his father, the Bishop of Winchester. North left the running of the Hospital to a chaplain and a steward, but missed no opportunity to extract revenue from the Hospital's property. Vilified by the Press, he survived an investigation by the Ecclesiastical Commissioners, and was only removed in 1855 after a lengthy and costly court action. Estimates of what North appropriated from the Hospital vary from £50,000 to £250,000, but one thing is certain – he had destroyed the Hospital's wealth and left the buildings in serious disrepair. The scandal inspired Trollope's novel *The Warden*.

It was a forbidding situation for the new Master, L.M. Humbert. But he revelled in the challenge and much of the credit for the restoration of St Cross and the build-up in public confidence in the institution is due to his endeavours. Although faced with immense problems after so much neglect, Mr Humbert was not without a sense of humour. Five years after the Earl of Guildford's resignation, Mr Humbert wrote to him pointing out that St Cross was short of silver. Perhaps, he enquired, the Earl would like to donate a silver chalice in memory of his connection with St Cross. The Earl, by this time nearly 88 years old, was not amused.

Over the last 100 years St Cross has recovered spiritually and materially giving us today the very special atmosphere here that Henry de Blois intended.

ABOVE: *This and similar panels on subsequent pages contain lines from the poem, written in 1763 by William Long, from the wall of the Brethren's Hall.*

BELOW: *A mid-19th-century photograph of the Master and Brothers. The title of 'Master' gradually replaced 'Prior' towards the end of the 12th century, to distinguish St Cross from ecclesiastical institutions. At about the time of the photograph a board of trustees became responsible for the Hospital's administration.*

Visitors to St Cross Hospital enter through the outer quadrangle, passing on their right the former guest wing and on their left the old brewhouse, site of the '**Hundred Men's Hall**'. The original hall used to stretch further towards the inner gate, and was where, under the terms of Henry de Blois' foundation, a hundred poor men came daily for their dinner. A man's daily ration was considerable – '3 quarts of small beer, a loaf of bread and two messes (stews)', a reflection of the fact that this allocation also fed his family.

The **Beaufort Tower** (*c*.1450) guards the entrance to the inner quadrangle. It was built by Cardinal Beaufort, the immensely powerful Bishop of Winchester (1404–37) who can be seen praying in the sole remaining statue on the outer wall. Where the porter now issues the Wayfarer's Dole was once the entrance to the Master's lodging. His rooms above and to the east of the arch were linked to the church by the **ambulatory** or cloister which runs along one side of the quadrangle. In spite of its appearance this building, with its timbered first-floor gallery, is the youngest part of the hospital. It is thought that the first floor was intended as an infirmary.

On the west side of the quadrangle is the range of **Brother's quarters**, distinctive for the tall external chimneys. Each of the doorways leads to four quarters, two on each floor. Beyond these, on the south side, the view to open fields marks the site of the original almshouses and a choirboys' school, pulled down in the 1760s because of their dilapidated condition.

On the north side of the quadrangle stands the **Brethren's Hall**, where the Brothers formerly gathered. This atmospheric room with its fine roof made of

BELOW: The Brethren's Hall, where Brothers lived and fed for several centuries. In the centre is the open hearth where a charcoal fire burned. Its smoke did not escape but drifted up to disperse in the rafters.

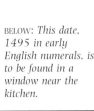

RIGHT: The ambulatory stretches from the former Master's lodging to the church.

BELOW: This date, 1495 in early English numerals, is to be found in a window near the kitchen.

Spanish chestnut, built as the Master's hall *c.*1340, is remarkably preserved. The Brothers moved in when the Master's lodging was moved in the later 16th century.

Almost all the hall's original features are still here today, the central hearth where a charcoal fire used to burn, the stairs leading direct from the Master's lodging, the raised platform where he took his meals at the high table and the musicians' gallery. High up in the wall at the east end was a window from which the Master could keep an eye on proceedings. The heavy oval table of Purbeck marble which stands in the far corner dates from the 12th century and is thought to have come from Winchester Castle.

The hall is the scene of the Gaudy Lunch (from the Latin *gaudere*: to rejoice), traditionally held several times a year with no higher aim than to bring the Brothers together to enjoy a large convivial feast. These days the lunch takes place three times a year.

Here hoary Age disconsolate and forlorn,
Midst fortunes frowns may cease its fate to mourn
And here may sit devoid of every care,
Save what a mortal State must ever share.
O blest retreat! retir'd from noise and strife,
Could I but spend the Evening of my Life
Within these Courts, within this hallow'd Dome
Could wait a Passage to the silent Tomb;

ABOVE: *The large size of the kitchen reflects the fact that it did not feed just the 13 Brothers in the adjoining hall, but also the 100 men who came to dinner every day. A door just out of the picture to the right led to the outer quadrangle and the Hundred Men's Hall on the opposite side.*

Beyond the hall is the impressive kitchen, which remained in day-to-day use until the late 19th century. The fireplace dates back to the 15th century; the rotating spit, the bread oven and the copper for heating water were introduced later.

Around the kitchen are utensils, pewter dishes and flagons which are many centuries old. Brothers drank their beer from the 15th-century black leather jacks now on display. The room adjacent to the kitchen was a meat store and in the cellar beneath it, we can see where the barrels of beer were racked.

The fine Transitional Norman church is the only major survival from the Hospital's earliest days. It is also the centre of worship for the parishioners of St Faith's, but they are allowed in only as long as the Brothers have their places reserved.

Building was started in *c.*1135 at the east end. The north porch was not begun until well into the 13th century. It was completed under Peter de Sancta Maria in 1295. The walls are over 3 feet (1m) thick, of stone from Caen, Dorset and the Isle of Wight combined with flint from local chalk pits.

Originally thatched, the church acquired a lead roof at some time between 1335 and 1345 while William de Edington was Master. The west window and the clerestory windows date from the same time. John de Campeden made many changes to the building between 1383 and 1385, raising the tower and reroofing the choir.

The altar stone, from de Campeden's time, spent several hundred years beneath the altar, only being restored to its former position in 1928. It is thought that the Hospital was warned in advance that Cromwell's Puritans were planning to visit and had enough time to save the stone by burying it.

The medieval encaustic tiles (*c.*1390), seen at their best near the font, are very similar to those in Winchester Cathedral. It is thought they were made either at Romsey or Poole. In the north transept a square panel bearing the Hospital's badge and its motto 'Have mynde' shows how these tiles were produced by filling indentations in terra cotta with a separate glaze.

BELOW LEFT: *This magnificent building is reputed to be one of the finest examples of Transitional Norman church architecture in the country.*

BELOW RIGHT: *Services have taken place in the church every day for over 800 years.*

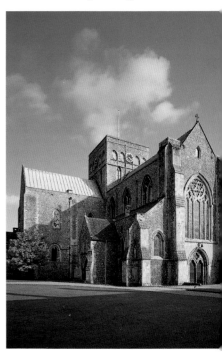

LEFT: *One of the church's oldest windows in the south transept, depicting St Gregory.*

RIGHT: *The Lady Chapel. The triptych is Flemish, bought on the continent for £80 by a former Master. The Beaufort chair on the left is brought out and used at the gowning ceremony of a Brother.*

> *Here would I contemplate all Nature's Laws,*
> *Adore her Beauties and her first great Cause;*
> *And daily offer in this sacred Fane,*
> *My grateful Tribute to my Maker's name.*

At the side of the organ in the south transept, traces of wall paintings in a tomb recess are the last remains of what was once an altar to St Thomas of Canterbury, the martyred archbishop. A nearby door was where travellers coming from the continent to Canterbury arrived. It would also have been the point of departure for crusaders. Knights of St John would spend their last night praying here before embarking at Southampton for the Holy Land.

Several features of the church were brought from the nearby church of St Faith's, demolished in 1507. Most prominent of these are the Norman font and the stone screens on either side of the sanctuary. The ornate wood carving in the choir is thought to have come from Wolvesey Palace at the time of Bishop Fox. (The pelican is his emblem.) These screens contain the carved head of Queen Anne Boleyn. One story is that Henry VIII, shortly after having Anne beheaded, was due to visit the Bishop, who anxiously removed anything that might have incurred royal displeasure.

BELOW: *Examples of ancient graffiti, from the stalls of the Beaufort foundation on the north side of the choir.*

> *… there are five Festival days in the year, to wit, – All Saints, Christmas, New Year's day, Twelfth day, and Candlemas day; on which the brethren have extraordinary commons, and on the eve of which days they have a fire of charcoal in the Common hall, and one jack of six quarts and one pint of beer extraordinary to drink together by the fire. And on the said Feast days they have … a sirloin of beef roasted, weighing forty-six pounds and a half, and three large mince-pies, and plum broth, and three joints of mutton for their supper.*
>
> MARKLAND'S CUSTOMARY 1694

Although the origins of St Cross Hospital are ancient, it is by no means a museum piece, but rather a thriving community of warmth and enthusiasm, acting as sheltered accommodation for 25 elderly men. Interpretations of a Brother's duties and entitlements have varied over the years, but life at the Hospital today is carried on very much according to the terms of the original foundation.

Traditionally, a Brother's duties are to attend a morning service daily, if well enough to do so, and to wear the gown, whose design dates back to the

RIGHT: *Tradition holds that the newest Brother summons his colleagues to the Friday pay parade.*

BELOW: *The Brothers' bowling green was situated beneath the east window of the church. Note the various hats on display.*

Knights Hospitallers. There are up to 17 Brothers from the original Foundation, who wear a black gown with a silver cross, and up to eight Brothers of the Order of Noble Poverty, who wear a red gown with a cardinal's badge. In the past, a variety of headgear has been permitted but since World War I only the original soft hat, or trencher, has been worn. In theory the gown should be worn all the time but over the last 30 years the rules have relaxed.

Some Brothers act as Exhibitors (guides) and others have duties in connection with the church. Brothers contribute towards their keep according to their means. They are provided with a one-bedroom flat, or quarter, with a

separate shower room and kitchen. Centuries ago, the lodgings would have seemed luxurious in the extreme. To have a second room was a great rarity but to have the heating of a coal fire …! The scale of provision was very different too (see panel above). These days Brothers are provided with a lunch if they wish to take it. The cosy little dining

other people coming in – a cook and a nurse daily, barbers and chiropodists every few weeks.

One tradition which endures is the weekly payment to each Brother of a small sum of money, probably in lieu of a coal allowance. These days it is £1. When the newest Brother rings a hand-bell all the Brothers gather in the old Master's Lodgings. The Receiver throws the money in leather purses across the table to each Brother assembled there.

When a Brother dies, the tradition used to be that he was buried with his cross and his trencher. In modern times these are left with the body until just before burial, when they are placed in the Master's safekeeping to be passed on to a new Brother.

To become a Brother, a man has to be 60 or over, of good character and able-bodied. There are no other formal qualifications and today's Brothers come from all walks of life and all parts of the country.

The 'gowning' ceremony is as it was centuries ago. Brothers are gowned by the Master at morning service, receiving a black or red gown according to the foundation of the Brother in whose steps they are following.

room that they use now is a far cry from the cavernous Brethren's Hall that was used for so many centuries.

In wealthier times, there would have been over 40 Hospital servants. These days a resident matron looks after the Brothers' welfare, with support from

ABOVE: *The Brothers' quarters with their distinctive external chimneys, built tall to improve the draught.*

LEFT: *The Brethren's Hall being used for its traditional purpose. A Gaudy Lunch is held in the hall three times a year.*

RIGHT: *A Brother of the Hospital foundation in his gown and trencher after the Friday pay parade.*

The Wayfarer's Dole

The Hospital of St Cross is famous worldwide for its unique and ancient tradition of the Wayfarer's Dole, a drink of beer and some bread given to visitors who request it.

The founder was a Cluniac monk and his order always gave bread and wine to travellers. The dole reflected this tradition, originally consisting of a bottle of wine and a loaf of bread!

These days lorries and cars thunder past on the nearby M3. In far-off days St Cross stood on an important east/west route. Pedlars with pack mules and pilgrims on ponies ambled through the water meadows to break their journey at the Hospital, resting tired horses and weary feet, and receiving refreshment, honestly requested and willingly given.

BACK COVER: *The view from the porter's lodge that greets all visitors to St Cross.*

RIGHT: *Two visitors receive their dole – 'a morsel of bread and a horn of beer' in the traditional receptacles, made from a cow's horn and hoof.*

BELOW: *The Hospital from the south-west. This looks across land where once stood a range of almshouses, demolished in the 1760s.*